INSTRUCTOR'S MANUAL TO ACCOMPANY

BREAKING THROUGH COLLEGE READING

Sixth Edition

Brenda D. Smith

Georgia State University

Longman

New York   San Francisco   Boston
London   Toronto   Sydney   Tokyo   Singapore   Madrid
Mexico City   Munich   Paris   Cape Town   Hong Kong   Montreal

NOTE REGARDING WEBSITES AND PASSWORDS:

If you need a password to access instructor supplements on a Longman
book-specific website, please use the following information:

Username: awlbook
Password: adopt

Senior Acquisitions Editor: Steven Rigolosi
Supplements Editor: Donna Campion
Electronic Page Makeup: Lorraine Patsco

Instructor's Manual to Accompany *Breaking Through: College Reading*, by Brenda D. Smith

Please visit our website at: http://www.ablongman.com

ISBN: 0-321-05105-x

12345678910-DM-03020100

CONTENTS

OVERHEAD TRANSPARENCY MASTERS

PREFACE

This book is designed to help students develop learning strategies to achieve success in college reading, and to transfer those successful learning strategies to other college courses.

ORGANIZATION OF THE CHAPTERS

Breaking Through opens with a chapter that describes the motivation, the actions, and the "mind set" needed for success in college. Chapter Two concentrates on theories of reading and the strategies used by good readers. Reading is thinking and interacting with the printed page in three stages: before, during, and after the process.

Chapter Three is dedicated entirely to vocabulary development, introducing and providing exercises on vocabulary building strategies such as using context clues, word parts, the dictionary, the glossary, the thesaurus, and analogies.

The most important reading comprehension skill is understanding the main idea. Chapter Four contains many practice exercises that move from the general to the specific in explaining this skill. Chapter Five reinforces the main idea skills with models, explanations, and practice exercises on the recognition of significant details, patterns of organization, and the beginning stages of note-taking. Chapter Six focuses on reading to learn and explains annotating, notetaking, outlining, and mapping.

Awareness and practice can improve test scores and give a winning edge. Chapter Seven helps students become aware of how tests are constructed and what is expected in the test-taking situation. It provides opportunities for application and practice.

Chapter Eight, on efficient reading, includes exercises to assess student reading rates and presents techniques for rate improvement. The characteristics of good students are again discussed in Chapter Nine, with an emphasis on the college student as an analytical reasoner and problem solver. Exercises are provided to help students develop and refine their analytical reasoning skills. Chapters Ten and Eleven explain implied meaning and focus on unstated attitudes and assumptions. These two chapters are designed to help students become more critical of what they read and more aware of suggested meaning and how writers can manipulate their audiences.

Success in college depends on the student's ability to transfer reading skills to daily textbook assignments in college courses. Chapter Twelve challenges the student to transfer skills, to study content, and to demonstrate learning in two textbook selections.

Each chapter is designed to be a self-contained teaching unit so that instructors can skip around and teach the skills in the order that best fits their needs. One chapter is not necessarily dependent on another, although some follow more logically than others.

ORGANIZATION WITHIN EACH CHAPTER

Most chapters follow a similar format. A reading skill is introduced and discussed, and short exercises are presented for practicing the skill. Then the new skill is applied to longer selections from college textbooks. The textbook passages are usually arranged from low to medium to high difficulty, with the first selection the easiest. Answers to the exercises appear in the Annotated Teacher's Edition.

The selections are followed by comprehension and vocabulary questions, as well as other open-ended questions for written responses. The comprehension questions ask for literal and inferential meaning and are designed to promote an understanding of the passage. The vocabulary words are listed in the phrases in which they appear. A line number is listed to note where the word appears in the selection so the student can refer to the larger context. In this edition vocabulary enrichment activities have been added at the end of the longer selections to reinforce the skills presented in Chapter Three. The longer selections also contain an Internet activity to motivate students to seek additional information on the subject.

The pages of the book are perforated so that students can tear out assignments and give them to the instructor for further evaluation. Responses to the reflection, essay, and summary items particularly need the individual attention of the instructor.

Preview Items

Always introduce and overview assigned readings. Use the preview questions to stimulate interest and to activate schemata. Remember that prior knowledge is the strongest predictor of reading comprehension. Corroborate for students that they do indeed know something about or related to the subject and help them realize that they must bring their own experience and knowledge to the printed page.

Written Response Items

The "React," "Reflect," and "Think Critically" questions following the selections offer opportunities for written responses. The "React" questions are positioned directly after the reading to encourage students to immediately recall and interact personally with what they have read. The "Reflect" items probe for the significance of the information, and the "Think Critically" questions explore the application of the material to other situations.

Connecting And Reflecting

Some of the longer readings have "Connect" passages at the end of the selections that are designed to encourage students to apply the reading to their own lives and to link old and new ideas. If used as an opportunity for collaborative learning, the passages can help students network knowledge, as well as network with each other.

Vocabulary Development

In addition to Chapter Three on vocabulary building, the vocabulary items at the end of each selection, and the vocabulary enrichment exercises, the *Instructor's Manual* contains True-False vocabulary items that can be used to stimulate thought before reading or to provide feedback after reading and studying the words.

Everyday Reading Skills

At the end of each chapter is a new section that focuses on reading needs students encounter in daily life. The topics include print media, electronic media, contemporary fiction and nonfiction, mnemonics, workplace reading, personal mail, and reference works. The purpose of these sections is to apply general reading skills to everyday life situations and provide students the strategies to become enlightened consumers and critical thinkers.

Collaborative Problem Solving

Four questions appear at the end of each *Breaking Through* chapter to provide collaborative applications and critical thinking opportunities that reflect the content of the chapter. Challenge students toward intellectual contributions. These activities can be motivating, stimulating, enlightening, and entertaining. Prior to assigning the activities, discuss group dynamics. Explain the characteristics of responsible leadership and group membership. Several enlargements on these topics are included in this Instructor's Manual for transparencies to assist you in classroom discussions.

I urge you to insist that each group uses a transparency for recording ideas to promote focus and clarity. After allowing group discussion time, ask one speaker or the total group to stand before the class and report the responses. Watch the time carefully to be sure that each group has the opportunity to report.

You can provide the transparencies and markers, or you can require that students purchase them at the bookstore when buying textbooks. The transparency method forces group decision making because of the need to get something written down to create the visual aid. During the presentation, the transparency provides a level of organization that does not always occur when students speak. The method also gives students practice in a lifelong business skill for successfully presenting material to groups.

Explore the Net Search

Most of the longer reading selections in Breaking Through end with Internet exercises that expand on the textbook topic and promote practice and proficiency in exploring the Internet. The Everyday Reading Skill at the end of Chapter One explains the steps in conducting a search and leads students through organized models of searching when Web sites are unknown. Since the listed Web sites are subject to change or obsolescence without notice, it is important that students know how to conduct their own searches.

Reader's Tip Boxes

These boxes condense strategies for improving reading and studying into practical hints for quick reference. An enlarged version of each box is included in the Instructor's Manual for you to copy onto a transparency for classroom presentations. Tips for reading and studying in specific college disciplines are inserted directly before the first longer selection in that particular discipline.

Vocabulary List

In order to provide a quick reference, the vocabulary words that are included in the questions at the end of each longer reading selection are listed in alphabetical order at the end of the textbook.

Readability Levels

With some exceptions, the selections in the chapter are on three different levels and progress from easy to more difficult readability. This arrangement gives the instructor flexibility both in assigning the selections and offering students work according to individual ability.

The Edward Fry Readability Formula was applied to the selections. To determine a grade level based on Fry's graph, the number of sentences and syllables are counted in three 100-word sections and averaged. Specific levels for all selections in the text are listed below.

Keep in mind that student interest can be far more important than readability level. If a student is interested in a passage, the material will seem easy and vice versa. You can help students overcome readability challenges with pre-reading activities that activate schemata and stimulate curiosity. For most of our students, college textbook reading is very difficult.

Grade Level Readability Scores For Selections

Variety of Content Area Materials

The selections were chosen to represent a typical variety of college courses. The content areas are represented as follows:

Psychology

Business

English (Essays and Short Stories)

Biology

Sociology

History

Communications

ADDITIONAL QUIZZES IN THE *INSTRUCTOR'S MANUAL*

The *Instructor's Manual* contains a short true-false quiz on comprehension and vocabulary for each longer reading selection. In some cases, the comprehensive questions are not very difficult and students may be able to answer them without reading the passage. On the other hand, some of the questions demand a thorough reading. Depending on the selection, you might use the questions in any of the following ways:

1. As a preview to be used before reading the selection.
2. As a method of beginning class discussion.
3. As a check to see whether students read and understood the selection.

Regardless of your purpose in using the questions, I suggest that on some occasions you call them out orally to help students sharpen their listening skills. Tell students that you will say a question once, repeat it once, and will not go back. The first two or three times you do this, a few students will ask you to repeat. Tell them you are sorry but you can't. After that they will listen more attentively and understand the questions the first time around. If you use the questions orally, for the sake of time you may want to pick only five of the comprehension and five of the vocabulary questions.

If time is an issue, the questions can be distributed. In this edition the questions are arranged on a separate page so that you can copy them for a class quiz or for individual students. When using the copier, fold back the answers. Be sure to collect the questions from students so that the quizzes do not "float."

Quizzes For Textbook Assignments

The *Instructor's Manual* includes tests for the two longer college selections in Chapter Twelve. These selections can be used to monitor the progress of students during the course and to assess their ability to transfer their skills to course work. Some instructors might want to use the selections as a midterm and a final exam.

Overheads for Class Discussion

Several pages are included that can be copied on transparencies and used on an overhead projector to direct class discussion.

PERSONAL FEEDBACK CONNECTION

Retention research has shown that success in college is not just about academics; it is also about the personal well-being of each student. Many freshmen orientation programs, for example, stress the importance of students finding a "significant other" adult on campus who can serve as a mentor and friend. Thus, my purpose in including the Personal Feedback questions is more personal than academic, although the questions are a mix of both. If students will respond in a serious manner, the answers can offer the instructor a wealth of information on the personal and academic struggles of each student. Even if you are not particularly comfortable with some of the questions, I encourage you to try them and see if the answers help you help your students. To encourage responses, I give students 5 to 10 points for answering each assigned page, and I assign enough sections to total 100 points. I then use this grade as a quiz or test grade.

Learning Tools in *Instructor's Manual*

Introductory Classroom Materials.   Samples for a number of introductory classroom materials are included in this Instructor's Manual, based on material that I have used in the classroom. These materials are included to serve as models and may or may not reflect the needs of your curriculum. Please feel free to copy these materials and adjust them to your own institutional and curriculum needs. The materials include the following:

Syllabus.   A sample syllabus is included in the *Instructor's Manual* to provide a possible model for developing your own syllabus. Change the specifics to fit institutional differences and your own course requirements. You may also want to develop a daily assignment plan for students to accompany your syllabus.

Operating Rules for the Classroom.   In order to be sure that students understand my expectation and are briefed on issues of civility, I have them sign this sheet and return it to me. I give them an additional copy to keep in their notebooks. I have found that an initial discussion of civility issues can prevent problems as well as lay the groundwork for behavioral consequences.

Sample Grade Sheet.   Students record and keep all their grades throughout the course on a grade sheet. This is done to make them feel more responsible about grades and to insure that they always have all the information that I have about their grades. These sheets are maintain by students (with reminders from me about recording), kept in their notebooks, averaged on the last day of class, and returned to me. Naturally, I also keep my own record of student grades.

A grade sheet model is included for you to use as a guide to reflect the requirements and percentage values in your own curriculum. In designing a grade sheet for your class, use the organization to indicate the percentage of value for each of your major grading categories. Within each major area, if you are unsure of the number of daily homework grades and quizzes, insert more than enough blanks for grades. I have never had a student complain about completing fewer assignments.

Sample Mid- Semester Evaluation Form.   Feedback from a mid-semester evaluation can be rewarding and informative. The timing works in your favor and gives you the information to insure that students end the course with a positive experience. This feedback allows you to find out about individual concerns, address them, and make appropriate changes that can strengthen the course.

Sample Feedback Form for Presentations.   If you assign classroom presentation, you can distribute these forms so that each student, as well as yourself, can give constructive feedback in organized categories. Each of these categories should be discussed before the presentation.

Research Permission Form.   I have also included a permission form that students sign on the first day of class so that I can use student writing for research and professional presentations. Again, rules regarding this will vary among institutions.

Class Roster.   Circulate a sign-up sheet for names, phone numbers, and e-mails. Copy this information and distribute it to each class member. Use this to build a sense of community and to insure that students have contacts for assignments.

Effective Leadership and Group Membership Characteristics.   Using a transparency, discuss this material with students prior to group activities or immediately after the first group session.

Class Visitation Assignment.   To build student awareness and self confidence, assign a visit to a 100 or 200 level lecture course. Ask student to not only take organized notes on the lecture but also to take notes on student behaviors. Grades will be based on a combination of the reports on the two activities. A complete explanation of the assignment is included for you to distribute to students. I view this assignment as a capstone experience. I make it in the second half of the semester after completing instruction on main idea skills. Give students plenty of advanced notice so that they can select an appropriate class—which is an assignment in itself. Students who pick interesting classes love this activity, and those who don't learn about the value of investigation before registration. For your own course planning, consider that this is an excellent assignment to leave with students when you attend a professional conference. You can be assured of an active discussion upon your return to class.

Assessment Test Package

This package includes six objective reading tests to measure student progress. Depending on the level of your students, two tests are available on three different levels of reading: beginning, middle, and high. For Breaking Through, your students will probably need the beginning level, or perhaps the middle level. Within each level, one test could be used toward the mid term of your course and the other might be used toward the end. At the beginning level, both tests include main idea, inference, and vocabulary questions. At the middle and high levels, the first test has main idea, detail, and vocabulary questions, whereas the second test includes main idea, detail, inference, and vocabulary items.

Using Longman's Reading Ancillary Package with *Breaking Through*

Longman is proud to offer instructors and students a wealth of reading resources with *Breaking Through*. All of the following resources are available free or at greatly reduced prices.

Reading Road Trip CD-ROM.   For those with access to a computer lab, this innovative, exciting, and popular multimedia reading software package takes students on a tour of 15 cities and landmarks throughout the United States. Each of the 15 modules corresponds to a reading or study skill (for example, finding the main idea, understanding patterns of organization, and thinking critically). All modules contain a tour of the location, instruction and tutorial, exercises, interactive feedback, and mastery tests. A Reading Road Trip CD can be packaged free with *Breaking Through*. Ask your sales representative for more information.

The Dictionary Deal.   Handy as resources in general and useful in conjunction with Chapter 3 (Vocabulary), two dictionaries can be shrinkwrapped with any Longman Basic Skills title at a nominal fee. *The New American Webster Handy College Dictionary*, third edition (0-451-18166-2) is a paperback reference text with more than 100,000 entries. *Merriam Webster's Collegiate Dictionary*, tenth edition (0-87779-709-9), is a hardback reference with a citation file of more than 14.5 million examples of English words drawn from actual use.

The *Breaking Through* Website.   For those who have already integrated an electronic component into the reading curriculum and equally for those who plan to do so, the book's Website (**http://www.ablongman.com/smith**) offers a wealth of exercises, readings, Internet resources, real-time chat, and links to activities in *Breaking Through*. Visit the book's Website to see how well it complements the Explore the Net Search activities in each chapter. Activities and content are refreshed and updated on an ongoing basis.

The Longman Textbook Reader.   For those with a focus on cross-disciplinary readings, this free supplement offers five complete chapters from Addison-Wesley/Longman textbooks: computer science, biology, psychology, communications, and business. Each chapter includes additional comprehension quizzes, critical thinking questions, and group activities. Available FREE with the adoption of *Breaking Through*. 0-321-07808-X.

Newsweek **Alliance.**   For those whose reading courses focus on contemporary issues, a 12-week subscription to *Newsweek* can be shrinkwrapped with this Longman text. The price of the subscription is 57 cents per issue (a total of $6.84 for the subscription). Available with the subscription is a free "Interactive Guide to *Newsweek*"—a workbook for students who are using the text. In addition, Newsweek provides a wide variety of instructor supplements free to teachers, including maps, Skills Builders, and weekly quizzes. *Newsweek* subscription card: 0-321-04759-1. Interactive Guide: 0-321-05528-4.

The Pocket Reader, **First Edition, and *The Brief Pocket Reader,*** **First Edition.** For those with students who repeat their reading course or take a progression of reading courses, these inexpensive volumes contain 80 and 50 brief, fresh readings (1-3 pages each), respectively, on a variety of themes: writers on writing, nature, women and men, customs and habits, politics, rights and obligations, and coming of age. Also included in each volume is an alternate rhetorical table of contents. *The Pocket Reader* 0-321-07668-0. *The Brief Pocket Reader* 0-321-07699-9.

Penguin Quality Paperback Titles. For instructors who like to teach novels, a series of Penguin paperbacks is available at a significant discount when shrink-wrapped with *Breaking Through*. A list of relevant American and British Literature titles follows:

English/Literature

E. Albee, *Three Tall Women*
0-452-27400-1 $9.95 / $4.00

D. Allison, *Bastard Out of Carolina*
0-452-26957-1 $12.95 / $5.00

J. Alvarez, *How the Garcia Girls Lost Their Accents*
0-452-26806-0 $12.95 / $5.00

S. Bellow, *The Adventures of Augie March*
0-14-028160-6 $14.95 / $5.50

W. Cather, *My Antonia*
0-14-028327-7 $10.95 / $4.00

K. Chopin, *The Awakening*
0-14-039022-7 $7.95 / $3.00

D. DeLillo, *White Noise*
0-14-028330-7 $13.95 / $5.00

W. Golding, *Lord of the Flies*
1-57322-612-2 $12.00 / $4.50

N. Hawthorne, *The Scarlet Letter*
0-14-039019-7 $5.95 / $2.50

G. Hutner, *Immigrant Voices*
0-451-52698-8 $6.95 / $2.50

D. Hwang, *M. Butterfly*
0-452-27259-9 $10.95 / $4.00

M. Karr, *The Liars Club*
0-14-017983-6 $12.95 / $5.00

A. Kennedy, *The Rough Guide to the Internet
& WWW 1999*
1-85828-343-4 $8.95 / $3.50

J. Kerouac, *On the Road*
0-14-018521-6 $12.95 / $5.00

K. Kesey, *One Flew Over the Cuckoo's Nest*
014-004312-8 $12.95 / $5.00

S. King, *Misery*
0-451-16952-2 $7.99 / $3.00

M. Lavin, *In a Café*
0-14-118040-4 $13.95 / $5.00

G. Marquez, *Love in the Time of Cholera*
0-14-028164-9 $14.95 / $5.50

J. McBride, *The Color of Water*
1-57322-578-9 $12.95 / $5.00

A. Miller, *Death of a Salesman*
0-14-048134-6 $7.95 / $4.00

T. Morrison, *Beloved*
0-452-26446-4 $12.95 / $5.00

T. Morrison, *Sula*
0-452-26349-2 $11.95 / $4.50

T. O'Brien, *The Things They Carried*
0-14-014773-X $12.95 / $5.00

N. Postman, *Amusing Ourselves to Death*
0-14-009438-5 $12.95 / $5.00

M. Rose, *Lives on the Boundary*
0-14-012403-9 $12.95 / $5.00

M. Rose, *Possible Lives*
0-14-023617-1 $13.95 / $5.50

S. Rushdie, *Midnight's Children*
0-14-013270-8 $14.95 / $5.50

M. Shelley, *Frankenstein*
0-14-043362-7 $7.95 / $3.50

Sophocles, *The Three Theban Plays*
0-14-044425-4 $9.95 / $3.50

British Literature

J. Austen, *Pride and Prejudice*
0-451-52588-4 $4.95 / $2.00

J. Austen, *Persuasion*
0-14-043005-9 $5.95 / $2.50

A. Behn, *Oroonoko & Other Works*
0-14-043338-4 $9.95 / $4.50

H. Bloom, *Shakespeare*
1-57322-751-X $15.95 / $6.00

C. Brontë, *Jane Eyre*
0-451-52655-4 $4.95 / $2.00

E. Brontë, *Wuthering Heights*
0-14-043418-6 $6.95 / $3.00

J. Conrad, *Nostromo*
0-14-018371-X $8.95 / $4.00

D. Defoe, *Robinson Crusoe*
0-14-043007-5 $7.95 / $3.50

C. Dickens, *Great Expectations*
0-14-043489-5 $7.95 / $3.50

C. Dickens, *Hard Times*
0-14-043398-8 $6.95 / $3.00

T. Hardy, *Jude the Obscure*
0-14-043131-4 $7.95 / $3.50

Homer, *The Iliad*
0-14-027536-3 $15.95 / $6.00

Homer, *The Odyssey*
0-14-026886-3 $14.95 / $5.50

Shakespeare, *King Lear*
0-14-070724-7 $5.95 / $2.50

Shakespeare, *Hamlet*
0-451-52692-9 $3.95 / $1.50

Shakespeare, *Macbeth*
0-451-52444-6 $3.95/$2.00

Shakespeare, *Othello*
0-451-52132-3 $3.95/$2.00

Shakespeare, *Four Great Tragedies*
0-451-52729-1 $6.95 / $2.50

Shakespeare, *Four Great Comedies*
0-451-52731-2 $6.95 / $2.50

M. Shelley, *Frankenstein*
0-14-043362-7 $7.95 / $3.50

J. Swift, *Gulliver's Travels*
0-451-52219-2 $3.95 / $1.50

V. Woolf, *Jacob's Room*
0-14-018570-4 $9.95 / $4.50

To Reach The Author

If you have comments, suggestions, or need more information, call me at 404-233-1116. I would like to hear from you.

Brenda D. Smith

COVERAGE FOR THE TASP AND CLAST READING SKILLS PROFICIENCY TESTS

College students in many states are required to demonstrate proficiency on reading tests that include a variety of skills. The following list shows where the skills on two such tests, the TASP and the CLAST, are covered in *Breaking Through*.

General Test Taking Skills	Chapter 7

TASP (Texas Academic Skills Program)

Determine the meaning of words and phrases

Context clues	Chapter 3
Multiple meanings	Chapter 3
Figurative language	Chapter 10

Understand main ideas and supporting details

Explicit or stated main idea	Chapter 4
Implicit or implied main idea	Chapter 4
Recognizing supporting details	Chapter 5

Identify a writer's purpose, point of view, and intended meaning	Chapter 11

Analyze relationship among ideas

Organizational patterns	Chapter 4
Drawing conclusions	Chapter 10, 11

Use critical reading skills to evaluate written material

Stated and implied assumptions	Chapter 10
Fact and opinion	Chapter 11
Logic	Chapter 9
Validity of analogies	Chapter 11
Bias of writer	Chapter 11

Apply study skills

CLAST (Florida College Level Academic Skills Test)

Literal Comprehension

Critical Comprehension Skills

 # CHAPTER ONE: STUDENT SUCCESS

Success begins with a positive attitude and with the belief that success is attainable. Students of college reading usually need a little "pep talk" at the beginning of the course. Many come with a negative feeling about being there. They know they have failed to meet college reading requirements and are upset with themselves for having to take a remedial or developmental course. An instructor can help improve students' attitudes and self-images by talking about goal setting and relating success stories. Discuss famous people who have met with a great deal of adversity and examine what made them persevere. Talk about short term and long term goals and ask students to answer the following questions:

- What are my goals for the next six months?
- What activities will help me achieve these goals?
- What is the best use of my time right now?

To achieve success, students must be willing to sacrifice. Sacrifice is more strictly defined for some than for others. Discuss the obvious sacrifices of time and money, and then move to the not-so-obvious everyday sacrifices, like not talking on the telephone or not watching that additional TV show, that will make a difference in the long run.

As a teaching strategy, encourage students to visit a freshman lecture class and to take notes on both the lecture and the behavior of other students. Talk about the choices that students make. Discuss the possible consequences of behavior like missing class, arriving late, sleeping in class, and not taking notes. Ask students to predict the A and B students from their class observations and to explain their predictions.

Graduation Completion Plan

Ask students to plan the courses that they will take each term in order to graduate in two years or four to five years, depending on the type of institution. This activity will entail some research for students to learn the requirements in their majors.

Improving Self-Image

As an exercise to improve self-image, ask the students to list ten interesting things about themselves. Then ask them to share the list with a classmate, and have each write a statement to introduce the other to the class. To vary this activity, have each student use an overhead for outlining the information when introducing a classmate. You may want to suggest that students do outside reading on self-improvement. Such books tend to be easy to read and motivating. Many students have never been exposed to positive mental attitude books and find them quite inspiring. You may want to suggest some titles, although most students like to browse in a store and pick their own.

A Written Book Report

Asking for a report on a book read outside of class is an exercise in both sharing and summarizing. Students might enjoy oral, group, or written reports. I have frequently used the following format to help students organize their reports.

A written book report should be approximately four or five pages long. Reports on required reading for other courses should not be accepted. At the beginning of the report, students should indicate the book's title and author and whether it is fiction or nonfiction. The body of the report should cover the following questions, which should first be discussed with the students. The suggested points for each section of the report are also indicated.

Fiction

1. Purpose: Why did you read this book? (10 points)
2. Characters: What type of people are the main characters? (10 points)
3. Plot: What happens in the book? What is the climax? (50 points)
4. Meaning: What ideas is the author trying to make? (20 points)
5. Evaluation: Why did you like or dislike this book? (10 points)

Nonfiction

1. Purpose: Why did you read this book? (10 points)
2. Authority: What makes the author an authority on the information presented? (10 points)
3. Synopsis: What information is covered? (50 points)
4. Significance: Why does this information need to be recorded? Why is it important? If you read a self-improvement book, explain how it can help you improve you life. (20 points)
5. Evaluation: Why did you like or dislike this book? (10 points)

Work with students on time management, and explain how it relates to college success and business success. Reinforce the use of time charts by asking students to complete several throughout the course. Ask each student to buy a daily planner, as well as other appropriate equipment for success. Check periodically to encourage students to plan and act for success.

Interaction and personal reflection are my goals for students reading the selections in Chapter One. The questions at the end of the readings have no correct answers. The aim is to have students bring a part of themselves to the print and to allow themselves to be affected by the message. The following questions, which may be used either before or after reading, may help guide your discussion of each selection.

Think Success

Does success begin as an attitude?

Why do some people achieve more than others?

Plan for Success

Do you manage your time, or does your time manage you?

How can you get control of your day?

Act Successful

What makes people look successful?

How does a successful student act?

How do you act successful?

Networking

What is collaborative learning?

Is it wrong to study together?

What bonds students to their educational institution? Is it athletics, clubs, or academics?

Why do business people network?

Academic Behaviors

As a teaching strategy, encourage students to visit a freshman lecture class and to take notes on both the lecture and the behavior of other students. Talk about the choices that students make. Discuss the possible consequences of behavior like missing class, arriving late, sleeping in class, and not taking notes. Ask students to predict the A and B students from their class observations and to explain their predictions.

Personal Feedback

Use the Personal Feedback sections to help you learn about your students and to help them learn about themselves. Shared information promotes bonding which leads to your becoming a "significant other" adult on that student's success team. Ask students to use the perforations to turn the feedback pages in to you. You may want to give 5 to 10 points credit for each completed feedback sheet.

Explore the Net

The use of these activities will depend on the availability of computer technology to you and your students. You may want to set up a system of giving 10 to 20 points for activities completed by individual students or collaborative groups. Use the activities to encourage growth.

READER'S TIP
Time Savers

Using time wisely becomes a habit. Analyze your current problems according to the following principles of time management to gain greater control of yourself and your environment.

1. Plan. Keep an appointment book by the day and hour. Write a daily To Do List.
2. Start with the most critical activity of the day and work your way down to the least important one.
3. Ask yourself, "What is the best use of my time right now?"
4. Don't do what doesn't need doing.
5. Concentrate completely on one thing at a time.
6. Block out big chunks of time for large projects.
7. Make use of five-, ten-, and fifteen-minute segments of time.
8. Keep phone calls short or avoid them.
9. Listen well for clear instructions.
10. Learn to say "No!" to yourself and others.
11. Wean yourself from TV. Business executives do not watch soap operas.
12. Strive for excellence, but realize that perfection may not be worth the cost.

READER'S TIP
Making a Learning Schedule

Use your assignment calendar to devise a learning schedule. Mark important dates for this class.

- Enter all test dates and due dates for papers.
- Divide reading assignments in textbook and record as daily and weekly goals. Leave several days for study and review before tests.
- Record dates for completing extra reading.
- Analyze assigned projects and create daily or weekly goals.
- Designate dates for completing the first draft of written reports.

READER'S TIP
Limiting Your Search

- Enter **"AND"** or a + sign between each word of your search. For example, using the words *Apple Computer* for your search will turn up thousands of hits that include not only sites about the company, but also sites related to apple (the fruit) and sites about computers in general. Using *AND* in your key phrase (*Apple AND Computer*) will return sites that only contain both words in the phrase.

- Enter **"OR"** to broaden a search. *Apple OR Computer* will return sites that contain information about either apples or computers.

- Enter **"NOT"** to exclude items. *Apple AND Computer NOT fruit* will exclude sites that mention fruit and computers.

- Use quotation marks when you want only hits that contain the exact phrase such as "Apple Computer Financial Report for 2001"

READER'S TIP
Using Institutional Indexes

Indexes are *databases* that categorize articles according to topics for easy access. Check with your library for the following popular college databases which are paid for by your institution:

Galileo

Periodical Abstracts

Newspaper Abstracts

Lexis-Nexis Academic Universe

MLA Bibliography

ABI Inform

Psyc FIRST

Social Science Abstracts

ERIC

MEDLINE

CHAPTER TWO: STAGES OF READING

Students think of reading as having only one stage, the "during" stage. The goal of Chapter Two is to help students see that reading is an interactive, three-stage process in which they use prior knowledge in all three stages to construct meaning. Stress the importance of activating schemata and adding to the "computer chips" by being a model for your students through prereading, and postreading activities.

To gain metacognitive control, students need to know what good readers do. Do not just tell them. Research indicates that you must show them the five thinking strategies of good readers in order to see an improvement. Model these skills for your students. Many materials are appropriate for demonstrating, but I particularly like to use the *Reading for Understanding (RFU)* cards by *Science Research Associates (SRA)*. These cards have been around for a long time, but they are very well done. In modeling your own thinking as an expert reader on these short, two- or three-sentence items, you can show how all five strategies are used to make meaning.

Reading recall is difficult to command. It can be requested, but the demand may be overlooked and is rarely accomplished. To encourage recall, explain the importance of recitation and encourage them to connect the new information with the old and to evaluate its worth.

Ask students if they are "buying in" or "tuning out" after reading. The reaction or evaluation stage may be done subconsciously or not done at all. Help students to be aware of the need to react to text.

STAGES OF READING

- **Before**
    - Preview
    - Set Goals
    - Activate Schema

- **During**
    - Predict
    - Picture
    - Relate
    - Monitor
    - Correct

- **After**
    - Recall
    - React

FIVE THINKING STRATEGIES OF GOOD READERS

1. Predict
Make Educated Guesses

2. Picture
Form Images

3. Relate
Draw Comparisons

4. Monitor
Check Understanding

5. Correct Gaps in Understanding
Seek solutions to confusion

Selection 1: Hypnosis

Answer with T *(true) or* F *(false).*

Comprehension Quiz (for prereading or postreading)

F   ____   1. Brain waves under hypnosis and sleep are the same.

F   ____   2. A person can be hypnotized against his or her will.

T   ____   3. Surgeons have performed operations on hypnotized patients who felt no pain.

F   ____   4. Hypnosis cannot be used to make people do things they wouldn't do under normal circumstances.

T   ____   5. Through hypnotic suggestion, the subject can be compelled to do something when the hypnotist is no longer present.

Vocabulary Quiz (for prereading or postreading)

F   ____   1. If you focus attention on a problem, you have failed to take careful notice.

F   ____   2. A selective choice is made without discriminating.

T   ____   3. Distracting noises catch your attention.

T   ____   4. A suggestible person can be easily manipulated.

F   ____   5. The babble of a baby makes a complete sentence.

F   ____   6. If you speculate in the stock market you sell all of your holdings and do not buy more.

F   ____   7. A person under anesthesia has complete control of his or her body.

T   ____   8. A posthypnotic suggestion is made before the subject comes out of hypnosis.

T   ____   9. A thermostat can be used to regulate heat.

F   ____ 10. A squiggly pattern is composed of straight lines.

Selection 2: The Killers Are Coming! The Killers Are Coming!

Answer with T *(true) or* F *(false).*

Comprehension Quiz (for prereading or postreading)

F   ____   1. The killer bees hitchhiked to Brazil on plants.

F   ____   2. The African bees killed many of the Brazilian honeybees.

F   ____   3. The killer bees in California were imported for breeding by beekeepers.

F   ____   4. According to the passage the construction worker drove his tractor over the hive and was attacked.

T   ____   5. African bees increased flower production in orchards.

T   ____   6. Among the bees first imported, twenty-six African queen bees escaped the netted enclosure.

F   ____   7. The traits of the Brazilian honeybees were dominant over the African bees.

T   ____   8. The Africanized bees produce enough energy to travel thirty-five miles.

T   ____   9. The Africanized bees mature sooner than honeybees.

T   ____   10. The Africanized bees die sooner than honeybees.

Vocabulary Quiz (for prereading or postreading)

F   ____   1. From the year 2000 to the year 2030, only two decades will elapse.

T   ____   2. An invaded country is a land attacked by outside forces.

F   ____   3. Agitated children are peaceful and quiet.

F   ____   4. If you have a sluggish metabolism, you burn calories quickly.

T   ____   5. A zippier group of friends would be more lively and exciting.

T   ____   6. A preliminary medical test is done first rather than last.

F   ____   7. A dominant personality is quiet and retiring.

T   ____   8. Intruding thoughts interrupt concentration.

T _____ 9. A flying squadron can be composed of military airplanes or bees.

F _____ 10. Continuous rain stops and starts periodically.

Selection 3: Problems in the Schools

Answer with T *(true) or* F *(false).*

Comprehension Quiz (for prereading or postreading)

T   _____   1. The students at Malcolm X Elementary School wear uniforms.

T   _____   2. The Malcolm X school is located in the central city of Washington, D.C.

T   _____   3. According to the passage, television consumes more of young people's time than school.

F   _____   4. The staff at Malcolm X feel that the key to success is money.

F   _____   5. The quotes of the first-year college student indicate disappointment because of poor grades.

F   _____   6. According to the passage, sociologists tend to conduct research on college classrooms.

T   _____   7. Karp and Yoels found less female participation with male professors.

F   _____   8. Karp and Yoels found that females participated much more than males with female professors.

T   _____   9. Karp and Yoels found that only 10 percent of class time is spent in discussion.

T   _____   10. According to the passage, early in each course professors single out a few students for answering questions.

Vocabulary Quiz (for prereading or postreading)

T   _____   1. Epidemic proportions suggest that many people are affected.

T   _____   2. A room engulfed in smoke should definitely be vacated.

F   _____   3. A plague is a promise for a better and more prosperous future.

T   _____   4. An ignited barn is not a safe place for horses and cattle.

F   _____   5. Constructive remarks are critical without being helpful.

T   _____   6. Joining in marriage is an example of a commitment.

T   _____   7. Prestigious implies status and power.

F _____ 8. To hit a chord is to summarize an event.

T _____ 9. A sidetracked plan has veered off course.

T _____ 10. The dynamics of a group refers to the interactions of its members.

Reader's Tip
Reading and Studying Science

- Master a concept by explaining it in your own words.
- Draw your own biological structures and diagram the processes to reinforce learning them.
- Use illustrations as a reading and review tool before exams.
- Use chapter summaries as study checklists to be sure you have reviewed all the chapter material.
- Think like a scientist at the textbook web site by participating in virtual research activities.
- Use mnemonics to memorize. Remember the example, **M**any **P**eople **F**ind **P**arachuting **A**larming—to remember the five kingdoms which are monera, protista, fungi, plantae, and animalia.
- Know the theories you are applying in lab and their significance.
- Blend lecture, lab, and textbook notes.

Reader's Tip
Reading and Studying Sociology

- Use the chapter outline, learning objectives, and introductory anecdotes to stimulate your schema and curiosity before reading.
- Use the summaries, key terms, and discussion questions to review your learning after reading.
- Think broadly about society and social organizations. Search for the historical reasons for human behaviors and organizational structures. Make cause-and-effect connections between history, culture and social organizations.
- Compare and contrast customs and social behaviors across cultures.
- Remain open-minded and learn tolerance for cultural differences. Avoid biased value judgments. Think objectively and scientifically to evaluate the problems of society.

READER'S TIP
Reading a News Story

- ***Get an overview from the headline and photographs***
- Answer the 5 W's and the H.

    Who is the story about?

    What happened?

    When did it happen?

    Where did the event or events take place?

    Why did this event occur?

    How did this happen?
- Continue to read according to the amount of detail desired.

READER'S TIP
Reading a Feature

- How does the angle or focus of a feature story differ from that of a straight news story?
- How credible are the sources cited?
- Is it factual or sensationalized?
- Does the reporter show a bias?
- Does the reporter judge or do you decide?

CHAPTER THREE: VOCABULARY

We can force students to memorize words for a test, but how can we help them remember the new word forever? Ideally, students should be immersed in a whole new environment where they hear the words used frequently. This is how young children learn language. Realistically, we can't transplant our students, but we can talk about the new words and try to use them as often as possible.

Encourage students to use concept cards. As you will discover, some words are more appropriate than others for concept cards. However, even for a word like *transmit*, which can easily be remembered structurally by prefix and root, the card and a picture will form additional links to aid student memory.

Demonstrate how the concept cards can be made. Suggest a word, discuss its meaning and use, and ask students for vivid visualizations. Help them arrive at a phrase and an image that suggest the meaning of a word. The creative part is particularly difficult for some students. For class discussion, you may want to try the following phrases:

extinct animal

deceptive answer

prestigious address

UNLOCKING WORD MEANING

◆ Context Clues

Definition

Elaborating Details

Elaborating Examples

Comparison

Contrast

◆ Word Parts

Roots

Prefixes

Suffixes

◆ Glossary

Terminology of the discipline

Special meaning of familiar words

◆ Dictionary

Guide Words

Pronunciation

Spelling

Word Meaning

Parts of Speech

Word History

READER'S TIP
Using an Electronic Thesaurus

Your word-processing program probably has a thesaurus. In *Word Perfect*, for example, the thesaurus is found in the *Tools* pull-down menu, as one of the *Language* options. To use this, select the word for which you want alternatives by dragging the cursor over the word to highlight it and then clicking on the thesaurus. An array of words will appear, usually both in the *Meanings* box and in the *Replace with Synonyms* box as indicated in the figure below displaying alternatives for the word *right*. Click and highlight a different word other than *just* which is presently highlighted in the *Meanings* box, you will get a different array of synonyms. For example, click on the word *sane* in the following illustration and your synonym options will be *normal, rational sound, reasonable*, and *wise*. This one word *right* has forty-nine synonym alternatives on this computer thesaurus in *Microsoft Word*. By moving the down-arrow situated to the right of the word *claim*, you will uncover the word *Antonyms* and the words *wrong, incorrect, erroneous,* and *lenient* will appear as options. Thus, your computer thesaurus has many more words than appear at first glance. Search and choose an option that fits the context of your sentence.

READER'S TIP
Categories of Relationships for Analogies

Synonyms: Similar in meaning

Start is to *begin* as *end* is to *finish*.

Antonyms: Opposite in meaning

Retreat is to *advance* as *tall* is to *short*.

Function, use or purpose: Identifies what something does. Watch for the object (noun) and then the action (verb).

Car is to *drive* as *towel* is to *absorb*.

Classification: Identifies the larger group association

Mosquito is to *insect* as *gasoline* is to *fuel*.

Characteristics and descriptions: Shows qualities or traits

Sour is to *lemon* as *sweet* is to *sugar*.

Degree: Shows variations of intensity

Walking is to *running* as *cool* is to *frozen*.

Part to whole: Shows the larger group

Pupil is to *school* as *sailor* is to *navy*.

Cause and effect: Shows the reason (cause) and the result (effect)

Work is to *success* as *virus* is to *illness*.

READER'S TIP
Easily Confused Words

capital: city

capitol: building

cereal: breakfast food

serial: episode

cite: quote

sight: vision

site: place

aisle: row

isle: island

accept: receive

except: all but

angle: in math

angel: in heaven

birth: have a baby

berth: bed

stationary: fixed position

stationery: paper

vain: conceited

vein: blood vessel

your: ownership

you're: contraction of *you are*

READER'S TIP
Subscribing to a Mailing List

- Use a mailing list search engine such as http://www.liszt.com/, http://tile.net/lists/, or http://www.lsoft.com/lists/listref.html to find directories of mailing lists.
- Type in keywords or phrases appropriate to your interest or research needs to find specific mailing lists.
- To subscribe to a *Listserv* mailing list (the majority of mailing list found through these search engines will be of this type), send an e-mail to the desired Listserv. In the body of the e-mail, type: SUBSCRIBE NAME OF THE LISTSERV your name. Use your first and last name after the name of the listserv, and leave the subject line blank.

READER'S TIP
Posting on a Newsgroup

- Type in keywords and phrases appropriate to your topic of interest through a newsgroup search engine such as http://www.liszt.com/news/, http://www.deja.com/usenet, or http://www.aol.com/netfind/newsgroups.html.
- Explore the newsgroups that most closely relate to your search criteria by reading the newsgroup without posting for a while (known as "lurking") and by reading the newsgroup's Frequently Asked Questions (FAQ).
- Either post or subscribe to the newsgroup by clicking on the appropriate icon.

Multiple Meaning Mix

Unravel the confusion. Pronounce and define the words with multiple meanings.

1. The bandage was wound around the wound.

2. The farm was used to produce produce.

3. The dump was so full that it had to refuse more refuse.

4. We must polish the Polish furniture.

5. He could lead if he would get the lead out.

6. The soldier decided to desert his dessert in the desert.

7. Since there is no time like the present, he thought it was time to present the present.

8. A bass was painted on the head of the bass drum.

9. When shot at, the dove dove into the bushes.

10. I did not object to the object.

11. The insurance was invalid for the invalid.

12. There was a row among the oarsmen about how to row.

13. They were too close to the door to close it.

14. The buck does funny things when the does are present.

15. A seamstress and a sewer fell down into a sewer line.

16. To help with planting, the farmer taught his sow to sow.

17. The wind was too strong to wind the sail.

18. After a number of injections my jaw got number.

19. Upon seeing the tear in the painting, I shed a tear.

20. I had to subject the subject to a series of tests.

# CHAPTER FOUR: MAIN IDEA

If students can state the main idea and distinguish the significant supporting details, they have the major skills needed for successful college textbook reading. Answering the question, "What point is the author trying to get across?" includes all other skills, even inferential comprehension.

For each selection in this book, always ask, "What point is the author trying to get across?" Ask this question so often and about so many different things that it becomes second nature to your students to expect it.

Explain to students that the main idea must be stated in a sentence; anything else is a topic. For example, "Sex" is a topic. "Sex in College" is also a topic. But "Sex in College is Good" or "Sex in College is Bad" are statements of the author's main idea. The statements are vastly different from the topic. Again, "Sex in College" is not a point.

I find it very difficult to get students to state the main idea in a sentence. They can state the *topic* fairly easily. In textbooks, the topic is frequently in the title of the chapter or in the boldface print. I view identification of the topic as an application of Piaget's concrete stage of thinking. In asking a student to state the author's main idea, we are requiring a more abstract level of thinking. We are moving the student into Piaget's formal stage of operations. Research indicates that 50 percent of the freshman population comes to college in the concrete stage of thinking. It is no wonder that we have trouble getting our students to state an author's main idea and support it with a few significant details.

I frequently compare the main idea to a thesis statement for an English class theme. This connects writing and reading for them, particularly when the stated main idea is at the beginning or end of a passage.

QUESTIONING FOR THE MAIN IDEA

1. Establish the Topic

Who or what is this about?

2. Identify Key Supporting Terms

What are the important details?

3. Focus on the Message

What is the main idea the author is trying to convey about the topic?

READER'S TIP
Reading and Studying a Short Story

Ask yourself the following questions as you read a short story:

- How would you describe the main character? What other characters are well developed? What is the purpose of the "flat" characters? What do the characters learn? How do the characters change?
- What is the main conflict in the story? What are the steps in the development of the plot? What is the climax? What is the resolution?
- What is the theme of the story? What universal truth did you learn from the story?
- When and where is the story set? How does the setting affect the theme?
- Who is telling the story? How does this point of view affect the message?
- What is the tone of the author? What mood is the author trying to create?
- What symbols provide vivid images that enrich the theme?
- What is your evaluation of the author's work?

READER'S TIP
Reading and Studying History

- Know the *who, what, when , where*, and *why significant* for people, places, documents, and events.
- Seek to understand the cause and effect relationship between events and their causes, results, and consequences.
- Use timelines to familiarize yourself with chronologies to get an overall picture of parallel or overlapping events.
- Learn significant dates to provide a framework for grouping and understanding events.
- Look at maps of the region being studied.
- Distinguish between fact and opinion, and compare your conclusions with the historian's interpretation.

READER'S TIP
Selecting a Book

After locating a book that looks interesting, further investigate using these strategies.

- Read the book jacket. Do the quotes from reviewers seem valid or clipped out of context? Do the blurbs introducing the book entice your interest? Has the author written other books that you have enjoyed? If nonfiction, what are the author's credentials?

- Read the first page and at least one other page. Do you like the writing style? Is it comfortable for you to read? Does the first page grab your attention?

- If nonfiction, look at the illustrations and read the captions. Are you intrigued?

- If nonfiction, review the table of contents and scan the index. Is this material that you want to learn more about?

Selection 1: Sleeping and Dreaming

Answer with T *(true) or* F *(false).*

Comprehension Quiz (for prereading or postreading)

T   _____   1. During REM sleep the brain waves are similar to those of a waking period.

T   _____   2. Everyone dreams.

T   _____   3. Dreaming is good for your mental health.

T   _____   4. Dreams are often symbolic of daily life.

F   _____   5. REM sleep occurs in over 80 percent of the total sleeping time.

Vocabulary Quiz (for prereading or postreading)

F   _____   1. A person who is unconscious is not able to breathe.

T   _____   2. The statement, "He is, but he isn't" is a paradox.

T   _____   3. A new gas station should be convenient to customers.

T   _____   4. White is sometimes used to symbolize purity.

T   _____   5. A boy who bullies others is not usually popular with his classmates.

F   _____   6. Idling away your time is a good way to achieve success.

F   _____   7. Depriving a person of an education will usually help him or her get a better job.

T   _____   8. The authorship of a story is ascribed to the writer.

F   _____   9. A critical question is of little importance.

T   _____   10. Synchronized watches tell the same time.

Selection 2: The Scholarship Jacket

Answer with T *(true) or* F *(false).*

Comprehension Quiz (for prereading or postreading)

F _____ 1. Martha was the first member of her family to win the scholarship jacket.

T _____ 2. Coach Thompson thought Martha would be a good forward on the basketball team.

F _____ 3. Martha overheard an argument between her history teacher and the principal.

T _____ 4. Mr. Boone was dishonest.

T _____ 5. The scholarship jacket was awarded to the valedictorian of the class.

T _____ 6. Martha was given to her grandparents to raise because her father could not earn enough to feed eight children.

T _____ 7. Martha was fifteen years old.

F _____ 8. Martha's grandmother tried to talk Martha into playing on the basketball team.

T _____ 9. Mr. Schmidt said he would not lie or falsify records.

T _____ 10. Martha was very thin.

Vocabulary Quiz (for prereading or postreading)

T _____ 1. Agile fingers facilitate typing.

T _____ 2. An upsetting incident can lead to despair.

F _____ 3. Absentminded behavior is usually deliberate.

F _____ 4. A planned meeting is an unusual coincidence.

T _____ 5. An employment interview is not an appropriate time to fidget.

F _____ 6. A comic joke usually calls for a sound of dismay.

F _____ 7. To muster up an audience is to offend a group.

T _____ 8. A gaunt athlete usually would not need to lose weight.

T _____ 9. A vile tasting beverage would probably not be a best selling drink.

Selection 3: The Dream of Nonviolent Reform

Answer with T *(true) or* F *(false).*

Comprehension Quiz (for prereading or postreading)

F   _____   1. King's famous "I Have a Dream" speech was made at the Washington Monument.

T   _____   2. The gathering in Washington at which King made his famous speech was to celebrate the centennial of the Emancipation Proclamation.

F   _____   3. The speakers who presented before King at the Washington gathering had electrified the crowd.

T   _____   4. The words "Free at last!" are quoted from an old song.

T   _____   5. King went to Memphis for a garbage workers strike.

F   _____   6. Black Power militants requested that King come to Memphis.

T   _____   7. The demonstrations in Memphis had become violent before King's arrival.

F   _____   8. King was shot on the balcony of the Masonic Temple while making a speech in Memphis.

T   _____   9. Before his death in prison, James Earl Ray denied having shot King.

T   _____   10. The FBI harassed King in an attempt to indicated that he was under the influence of Communism.

Vocabulary Quiz (for prereading or postreading)

F   _____   1. Sweltering weather is cooler than usual.

F   _____   2. A centennial celebration marks 50 years of existence.

F   _____   3. Oppressive heat is easily tolerated.

F   _____   4. A podium is a chair that is positioned in the front row on a stage.

T   _____   5. A resonant voice is strong and forceful.

F   _____   6. A galvanized crowd is restless and unfocused.

T   _____   7. If justice prevails, spurious evidence should not lead to a conviction.

T _____ 8. Dire poverty is desperate and excessive.

T _____ 9. If romantic love is recanted, a breakup may likely follow.

T _____ 10. If you are compelled to dance, you feel the need to rise and move to the beat.

CHAPTER FIVE: SUPPORTING DETAILS AND ORGANIZATIONAL PATTERNS

The most common organizational format in college textbooks (except in history and literature texts) is to introduce and define a term or concept, and then give examples or elaborate. If students learn to recognize this pattern, they will be less intimidated by college textbook reading.

To introduce this chapter, bring some psychology, sociology, or business books to class, and show students how page after page follows a similar organizational pattern. Show them how most of the words in the biology book are defined in the text itself. As an assignment, ask students to bring in examples from textbooks in other courses and identify the predominant patterns of organization.

This chapter also reinforces the concept of *main idea*. Encourage students to mark this textbook so that they are more aware graphically of how the different parts make up the whole. Ask them to tear out the pages so that you can check and see that adequate, but not excessive, markings have been made. This is also a beginning stage of notetaking. Students can see how recognizing the organizational pattern can help them mark the text for later study.

To reinforce the first section on levels of importance, ask students to visit an Internet Art Shop and find two paintings that they would like to purchase if money were no object. The following website is well organized and should produce interesting results: Paintingsdirect.com.

Ask students to print the chosen paintings and to use at least three levels of classification to find each painting. The levels include the following: artist, style, country of origin, color, size, and price. They can be used in any level of importance according to the desires of the purchaser.

PATTERNS OF ORGANIZATION

♦ **Listing**

♦ **Definition with Examples**

♦ **Time Order or Sequence**

♦ **Comparison or Contrast**

♦ **Cause and Effect**

READER'S TIP
Distinguishing Major and Minor Details

To determine which details give major or minor support, first identify the author's main point and then ask yourself the following questions:

1. What details are needed to explain or prove the main idea? (These are major details that give primary support.)
2. What details are included just to make the passage more interesting? (These are minor details that provide a secondary level of support.)

READER'S TIP
Following Directions

- Change your mindset from normal reading and commit to a different kind of task.
- Read to get an overview so that you have a general idea of the task and can make a plan.
- Assemble the necessary equipment, estimate the time, and find a helper if needed.
- Read each step sequentially, and do as directed. Move from word-to-word and phrase-to-phrase for a clear understanding. Read aloud if necessary.
- Use numbers, letters and guide words such as *first, next, before, after, then*, and *now* to maintain sequence. Insert your own numbers if steps are not sequenced.
- Visualize the process. Consult the diagram. Draw your own diagram if none exists.
- Think logically and keep your goal in mind.

Reader's Tip
Patterns of Organization and Signal Words

Addition:
(providing additional information)

furthermore, again, also, further, moreover, besides, likewise

Cause and Effect:
(showing one element as producing or causing a result or effect)

because, for this reason, consequently, hence, as a result, thus, due to, therefore

Classification:
(dividing items into groups or categories)

groups, categories, elements, classes, parts

Comparison:
(listing similarities among items)

in a similar way, similar, parallels, likewise, in a like manner

Contrast:
(listing differences among items)

on the other hand, bigger than, but, however, conversely, on the contrary, although, nevertheless

Definition:
(initially defining a concept and expanding with examples and restatements)

can be defined, means, for example, like

Description:
(listing characteristics or details)

is, as, like, could be described

Generalization and Example:
(explaining with examples to illustrate)

to restate, that is, for example, to illustrate, for instance

Location or Spatial Order:
(identifying the whereabouts of objects)

next to, near, below, above, close by, within, without, adjacent to, beside, around, to the right or left side, opposite

Simple Listing:
(randomly listing items in a series)

also, another, several, for example

Summary:
(condensing major points)

in conclusion, briefly, to sum up, in short, in a nutshell

Time Order, Sequence, or Narration:
(listing events in order of occurrence)

first, second, finally, after, before, next, later, now, at last, until, thereupon, while, during

READER'S TIP
Reading and Studying Criminal Justice

- Identify criminal acts in legal terms. Make lists to commit to memory.
- Distinguish between the types of crimes and categories of criminals. Use charts to form groups.
- Know the legal behaviors and responsibilities required for making an arrest and gathering evidence. Make timelines.
- Understand the processes of the courts and the sequencing of legal actions. Create a flowchart for a visual display.
- Relate possible legal decisions and police actions to the balance of police powers and democratic freedoms.

READER'S TIP
Choosing a Magazine

- Read the lead article headlines and the table of contents to find articles of interest to you.
- Flip through the magazine and read article titles and boxed article excerpts.
- Use article subheadings to preview.
- Read the captions of photos that interest you.
- Read several *Letters to the Editor*.
- Decide, purchase, and enjoy!

Selection 1: Confidence Games

Answer with T *(true) or* F *(false).*

Comprehension Quiz (for prereading or postreading)

T   ____   1. According to the author, confidence artists prey on the frailties of human nature.

T   ____   2. According to the passage, many victims do not report confidence scams.

T   ____   3. In the pigeon drop, the victims must pay to share money that is found in a wallet or envelope.

F   ____   4. In the bank examiner scheme, the con artist goes with the victim inside the bank to withdraw money.

F   ____   5. In the inheritance scam, the victim receives the money but it is quickly taken away.

T   ____   6. In the three-card monte, the victim wins initially.

F   ____   7. In the C.O.D. scam, the person to whom the package is addressed is the one who pays the money.

F   ____   8. In the money-making-machine scam, American money is used to make German money.

T   ____   9. In the Nigerian oil con, the con artists place advertisements in newspapers to find victims.

F   ____ 10. In the Nigerian oil con, the price of oil quoted to the victim is less than half of the current market price.

Vocabulary Quiz (for prereading or postreading)

T   ____   1. The phrase, "annals of time" suggests the records of the past.

F   ____   2. Cunning crooks lack guile.

T   ____   3. Human frailties are weaknesses rather than strengths.

T   ____   4. A monetary reward is a cash payment.

F   ____   5. A swindle is a deal that is lawful and just.

F   ____   6. A sleight of hand is obvious to most onlookers.

T _____ 7. Fraudulent documents are created illegally.

T _____ 8. A phony driver's license is a fake identification.

T _____ 9. Affluent customers have spendable income.

F _____ 10. Perishable goods do not quickly spoil.

Selection 2: Becoming Healthy

Answer with T *(true) or* F *(false).*

Comprehension Quiz (for prereading or postreading)

F _____ 1. You can be healthy simply by deciding to be healthy.

T _____ 2. Self-doubt comes from a feeling that other people will not find you acceptable.

T _____ 3. Expressing your feelings to other people can reduce tension.

T _____ 4. Being loved is a health-producing experience.

T _____ 5. Other people help us define who we are.

Vocabulary Quiz (for prereading or postreading)

F _____ 1. A pervasive odor is easy to eliminate.

F _____ 2. Hikers usually want to encounter a bear while in the forest.

T _____ 3. Excessive drinking can lead to alcoholism.

F _____ 4. Timidity is a desirable quality in a public speaker.

F _____ 5. Human frailty is a sign of strength.

T _____ 6. A chronic illness seems to be with you all the time.

T _____ 7. A new perspective can be a different point of view.

F _____ 8. Profound sorrow is insincere regret.

T _____ 9. Sometimes competency is measured by a standardized test.

F _____ 10. To look at yourself in the mirror is an example of self-transcendence.

Selection 3: The Nature of Infectious Diseases

Answer with T *(true) or* F *(false).*

Comprehension Quiz (for prereading or postreading)

T _____ 1. AIDS is an example of a pandemic.

T _____ 2. According to the passage, *Ebola* may have evolved from monkeys in tropical forests in Africa.

F _____ 3. According to the passage, 50% of the infected humans recover from *Ebola*.

T _____ 4. According to the passage, with *Ebola* blood is free to seep out of the body.

T _____ 5. According to the passage, crowed cities enhance the possibility of spreading infectious diseases.

T _____ 6. *E. coli* can enter the system through undercooked beef.

F _____ 7. Animal manure can not contaminate vegetables.

T _____ 8. According to the passage, bacteria can live for two months in a wet sponge.

T _____ 9. According to the passage, kitchen bacteria can be killed with household bleach.

T _____ 10. According to the passage, *E. coli* can be contracted from unpasteurized apple juice.

Vocabulary Quiz (for prereading or postreading)

T _____ 1. Mobilized troops are moving toward conflict.

F _____ 2. When the tide subsides, the water is at its highest level on shore.

T _____ 3. To taxi a germ is to carry it to another location.

T _____ 4. The ears are orifices of the human body.

T _____ 5. A deranged patient does not act sensibility.

T _____ 6. When a task is implemented, the work is finally begun.

T _____ 7. Invincible warriors survive danger.

F _____ 8. A prominent facial feature is difficult to see.

F _____ 9. The culprits of a crime are the helpless victims.

F _____ 10. An ingested food never enters the body.

CHAPTER SIX: TEXTBOOK LEARNING

Reading for recreation and reading to learn involve two different purposes. Explain the differences and then begin a discussion of study strategies. Ask students how many times they have heard classmates say, "I really studied for my midterm exam; I read all the material three times." Talk about what happens during rereading and why it is not an effective study method. Point out the need in study reading to organize information to facilitate future learning.

After completing this chapter, you may want to assign one of the selections in Chapter 11 to assess transfer and independent learning. Each selection in Chapter 11 begins with notetaking or outlining models for further reinforcement. Students should choose their own strategy for finishing notes on the selection. Use the selection quizzes in this manual to motivate students to study their notes.

Six Types of Love

I. Eros: Beauty and Sensuality
   A. Focus: physical attractiveness
   B. Idealized and unattainable image of beauty
   C. Often unfulfilled
   D. Report highest levels of satisfied lovers

II. Lundus: Entertainment and Excitement
   A. Focus: a game to be played for fun
   B. Emotions and passion held in control
   C. Self-controlled and manipulative
   D. Report dissatisfaction with less happiness, friendship, and trust

III. Storge: Peaceful and Slow
   A. Focus: companion relationship with shared interests
   B. Lacks passion and intensity
   C. Develops over time and sex is late
   D. Mutual caring and respect

IV. Pragma: Practical and Traditional
   A. Focus: meet needs for a good life
   B. Concern over social qualifications
   C. Family, background, and job important
   D. Relies on logic rather than feelings

V. Manic: Elation and Depression
   A. Focus: has to possess the beloved completely
   B. Loves, worries, and fears intensely
   C. Obsessive and driven
   D. Wishes to be possessed

VI. Agape: Compassionate and Selfless
   A. Focus: self-giving love
   B. Love for strangers
   C. Spiritual love offered without gain
   D. Related to female life satisfaction

ORGANIZING TEXTBOOKS FOR LEARNING

- ◆ **Annotating**
- ◆ **Notetaking**
- ◆ **Summarizing**
- ◆ **Outlining**
- ◆ **Mapping**

READER'S TIP
How to Write a Summary

1. Remember your purpose; be brief.
2. Underline the key ideas in the text that you want to include.
3. Begin your summary with a general statement that unites the key ideas.
4. Include the key ideas that support the general statement. Link these ideas in sentences, and show their significance.
5. Delete irrelevant or trivial information.
6. Delete redundant information.
7. Use your own words to show your understanding of the material. Don't try to camouflage a lack of comprehension.

READER'S TIP
Defining Your Topic

To define your research topic, consider:

Geography: Pick a specific area.

Time Frame: Limit the time period under examination.

Interest Groups: Narrow your research by appropriate descriptors such as age, gender, or occupation.

Academic Discipline: What college or department would study this subject?

READER'S TIP
Reading and Studying Business

- **Business Profiles.** Activate your schema with the introductory profiles and boxed materials that describe an actual company with a current marketing dilemma involving the chapter concepts.

- **Theory and Practice Connections.** Connect business theories with a real company problem or solution to make learning easier. Use the business illustration to visualize the concept.

- **Illustrative Aids.** Cross-reference your reading with the illustrative photographs, tables, flow charts, figures, and copies of real advertisements. Consider these visual learning tools to enhance your learning.

- **Case Histories or Running Cases.** Apply theory to reality with the case histories. Sometimes these are a continuing story in each chapter about the same company's use of the chapter concepts. One textbook, for example, has a continuing story of the Harley-Davison Motorcycle Company and its rise to success. Other texts may have many different case studies ranging from the success of Fisher-Price in the competitive toy market to the ethical issues of increasing global marketing of tobacco products when the dangers of tobacco are clearly delineated here at home.

- **Computer Exercises.** Use the exercises to reinforce chapter topics, strengthen your research skills, and expand your knowledge. An instructional software disk may come with your text with practice quizzes and other instructional help.

- **Career Focus.** Use the tips that suggest how to "market" yourself by applying the chapter's concepts in your career search, For example, tips may offer advice on how to identify and access the major employment pipelines (*distribution channels*) for your product (you) in your career search.

Selection 1: Cesar Chavez

Answer with T *(true) or* F *(false).*

Comprehension Quiz (for prereading or postreading)

F   _____   1. Chavez migrated from Mexico to California when he was a teenager.

T   _____   2. Chavez attended over 30 schools as a migrant child.

T   _____   3. Chavez was a veteran of World War II.

T   _____   4. Chavez used his lifetime savings to create the National Farm Workers Association.

F   _____   5. The Community Service Organization supported Chavez's proposal to establish a farmworks union.

F   _____   6. The grape pickers that urged the 1965 strike were largely Mexican.

F   _____   7. Chavez's fasting lasted for 60 days.

F   _____   8. Chavez's fasting pressured growers into settling with the strikers.

T   _____   9. Chavez's efforts outlawed the short hoe.

T   _____ 10. Because of the strike, migrant workers won the right to bargain collectively.

Vocabulary Quiz (for prereading or postreading)

T   _____   1. An impoverished community needs aid and economic support.

F   _____   2. Little work would be needed on a dilapidated mansion.

T   _____   3. If you are shunted to a theater aisle, you are taken off your original course.

T   _____   4. A staunch Republican would seldom vote for a Democrat.

F   _____   5. Popular cosmetics are designed to produce a marred appearance.

F   _____   6. Pelting rain is only a very slight drizzled.

F   _____   7. Those who want continued fighting would seek to quell violence.

F   _____   8. An escalating conflict decreases in intensity.

T   ____ 9. Your heritage commemorates the past rather than the future.

T   ____ 10. A legacy can be a million dollar gift from you to your college.

Events Timeline for Chavez

1927	Born in Yuma, Arizona as one of five children of Mexican immigrants
1944	Joined navy and served on destroyer
1952	Joined the Community Service Organization and became general director in 1958
1962	Organized migrant grape laborers into the National Farm Workers Association
1965	Drawn into Filipino grape pickers strike
1966	Led 250-mile Easter march to dramatize plight of farm workers and merged with AFL-CIO
1968	Began fast to protest which did not get results
1969	Initiated a boycott of table grapes
1970's	Grape growers under union contracts
1993	Died at age of 66 having gained rights for workers

Selection 2: The Beanie Baby Business

Answer with T *(true) or* F *(false).*

Comprehension Quiz (for prereading or postreading)

T   ____ 1. Ty's first job after college graduation was with a stuffed animal company.

T   ____ 2. In lawsuits, companies producing knockoff Beanie Babies have been forced to give profits to Ty.

F   ____ 3. Ty Inc. uses television to advertise Beanie Babies.

F   ____ 4. The Ty Inc. sells collectable Beanie Babies for prices that can be over $1,000.

F   ____ 5. Beanie Babies are manufactured in the United States.

F   ____ 6. Beanie Babies are filled with beans.

F   ____ 7. At MacDonald's the free Beanie Babies with Happy Meals sold out in 35 days.

F   ____ 8. The author suggests that Ty Inc. opposes the secondary Beanie Baby market.

F   ____ 9. The author implies that Ty Inc.'s updated computer system allowed individual customers to place orders.

T   ____ 10. According to the passage, Ty Inc. has produced over 100 different Beanie Babies.

Vocabulary Quiz (for prereading or postreading)

T   ____ 1. A staggering number is an amazing amount.

F   ____ 2. Inevitable consequences usually never happen.

F   ____ 3. If you are involved in a craze, you reject a popular trend.

T   ____ 4. Obsolete machinery is no longer useful in a factory.

T   ____ 5. An obstacle to success is a hindrance in achieving progress.

T   ____ 6. Innovative ideas stray form the norm.

T   ____ 7. Acting deceptively implies secretive movements.

T   ____ 8. To forgo desserts is to say no to sweets.

T _____ 9. Police use handcuffs for the purpose of restraint.

T _____ 10. A meeting hall is a place to congregate.

Ty Warner's Keys to Success

    I. Sell to specialty gift shops, not mass marketers
      A. Longevity
      B. Pay promptly

    II. Manufacture in China to cut costs

    III. Create new computer system for ordering efficiency

    IV. Create perception of scarcity
      A. Provide stores with too few items
      B. Stop making items
      C. Wait for demand to increase

    V. Form alliance for free advertising

    VI. Price low for impulse buying

    VII. Sue makers of knockoffs

Selection 3: Mass and Serial Murder

Answer with T *(true) or* F *(false).*

Comprehension Quiz (for prereading or postreading)

T   _____   1. Mass murder involves killing several people at the same time.

F   _____   2. According to the passage, mass murderers usually escape.

F   _____   3. According to the passage, most mass murderers are mentally ill.

T   _____   4. According to the passage, studies indicate that mass murderers appear to be ordinary people.

T   _____   5. Serial murderers kill several people one at a time.

F   _____   6. The author agrees with the media that serial murder is an epidemic.

T   _____   7. According to the passage, most serial murders commit their crimes in only one city.

F   _____   8. According to the passage, serial murderers are more likely to be caught than mass murderers.

T   _____   9. Serial murderers stalk their victims and study their routine.

T   _____   10. According to the passage, during childhood most serial killers tortured dogs and cats for thrills.

Vocabulary Quiz (for prereading or postreading)

T   _____   1. The scene of a slaughter is a place of carnage.

T   _____   2. A lethal injection leaves little room for a recovery.

F   _____   3. Alienated children find comfort at home.

T   _____   4. An arsenal of guns is an accumulation of firearms.

F   _____   5. Charismatic leaders are seldom charming.

T   _____   6. A credible report is accepted as believable.

F   _____   7. To roam for a lifetime is to establish one permanent residence.

F _____ 8. An elusive animal is easy to locate.

T _____ 9. Bait is a lure for catching fish.

T _____ 10. Remorse is a feeling of grief or sadness.

Characteristics of Mass and Serial Murderers

I. Mass Murderers
    A. Killing a number of people at the same time
    B. Die at the scene
    C. Not mentally ill
    D. Extraordinarily ordinary
    E. Some disgruntled employees, family heads, pseudocommandos, or teams lead by charismatic leader

II. Serial murders
    A. Killing a number of people one at a time
    B. Illusive at not getting caught
    C. Stalk their victims and study their activities
    D. Win the victim's confidence
    E. Lure the victim into a trap
    F. Tortured animals for thrill or were abused as children
    G. Not mentally ill and appear normal

CHAPTER SEVEN: TEST-TAKING STRATEGIES

In this chapter I have tried to give test-taking advice and teach test-taking strategies in an interactive manner. The initial advice is common sense, but many students are unaware of the obvious results of these actions. I used the anecdotes to freshen the approach for the students. The purpose is to make them think and later react in a class discussion.

The comprehension skills are those that are taught throughout the text. This is a chapter that needs the explanations offered in the other chapters to make it complete. To reduce student anxiety, it is especially important to show them that comprehension questions are predictable. After discussing the major question types, bring in some standardized tests and ask students to identify the types. Particularly point out that only vocabulary and a few detail items can be answered without a clear understanding of the passage.

Chapter Seven needs a lot of class discussion and modeling. It is particularly difficult for students to write test items, but remember that the ability to write test items is not the ultimate goal. I use this strategy to give students insight into what is being done to them by the test makers. Create some of the items in class, and then have students write others while working in groups of three.

Most of the answers for the exercises in this chapter will come from the students themselves. Some responses will be better than others, but again the purpose is to sensitize rather than to train a test-writing professional. Most of this chapter is very appropriate for in-class group activities.

Major Question Types

♦ Main Idea

> The best statement of the main idea is...
>
> The best title is...
>
> The central theme or message is...

♦ Detail

> According to the author...
>
> According to the passage...
>
> The author states that...
>
> A person, term or place is...

♦ Implied Meaning

> The author believes or implies that...
>
> The passage suggests...
>
> It can be inferred that...
>
> It can be concluded that...

♦ Purpose

> The primary purpose of the passage is...
>
> The author's purpose is...

♦ Vocabulary

> As used in the passage, the best definition...

READER'S TIP
Types of Test Passages

Factual Passages

What? Science or history articles

How to read? Read for the main idea, and do not get bogged down in details. Remember, you can look back.

Author's Purpose?

- To inform
- To explain
- To describe

Example: Textbooks

Opinion Passages

What? Articles with a particular point of view on a topic.

How to read? Read to determine the author's opinion on the subject. Then judge the value of the support included, and decide whether you agree or disagree.

Author's Purpose?

- To argue
- To persuade
- To condemn
- To ridicule

Examples: Newspaper editorials

Fiction Passages

What? Articles that tell a story

How to Read? Read to understand what the characters are thinking and why they act as they do.

Author's Purpose?

- To entertain
- To narrate
- To describe
- To shock

Examples: Novels and short stories

READER'S TIP
Remembering Information

- Hook it to mental signs that are easy to remember.
- Link it to other information or indicators you already know.
- Sense it by touching, writing, or speaking.
- Rehearse it by writing it or speaking it to yourself.

 # CHAPTER EIGHT: EFFICIENT READING

The emphasis of this text is not on speed but on comprehension. In general, however, students tend to enjoy and profit from a little instruction in efficient reading techniques. You can determine how fast or slowly your students are reading by giving a timed test. A student who is reading easy material at 150 words per minute will have trouble reading college textbooks. Such a student needs to make an effort to read faster.

In introducing efficient reading techniques, help students put speed into perspective. Explain reading flexibility, and discuss various materials and purposes that require different reading speeds. Caution students to be sure that they understand that you are not advocating speed reading a biology or history textbook for a final exam.

The exercises on word recognition, word meaning, and phrase meaning are included primarily because they are fun to do and encourage quick thinking. Students enjoy doing them as a group and competing against each other, so I suggest using them as a class activity. In addition, timing an exercise is easier for the student if the instructor is calling out the time. Do this by calling out *start* and then the number of seconds in five-second intervals. When everyone is finished, discuss the answers, and then encourage the fast readers and the slow ones. There is no correct speed, but the following would be considered good:

Exercise 2	Word Recognition	40 seconds
Exercise 3	Word Meaning	60 seconds
Exercise 4	Phrase Meaning	40 seconds
Exercise 5	Pen as a Pacer	
	Natural Gas Safety	25 seconds
	Allergic Reactions	25 seconds
	Typing Keyboard	30 seconds
	Language Development	60 seconds
	That Wonderful You	65 seconds

Again, these speeds have no magic meaning. An appropriate speed is individual. It also depends on how often the student is correct. The exercises were designed to be fun and to focus attention on concentration and faster thinking. Use them to have a good time.

Using a pen as a pacer may be awkward at first for many students, but encourage them to try it. Again, doing the exercises in class can make them more fun and also gives students an opportunity to try a new technique with the supervision of the instructor.

READER'S TIP
Managing Workplace Reading

- Set priorities before reading.
- Strive to handle a piece of paper only once.
- Respond to it, discard it, or file it.

READER'S TIP
Reading Newsletters

- Read selectively. You may want to read all of the newsletter or none of it.
- Read critically. You cannot consider the information in a newsletter to be objective since it contains information that is beneficial only to the company or organization. Unflattering information is not included, so the coverage is not balanced.
- Note items that are highlighted, set off by numbers, bullets, capital letters, or that appear in boldface or italic type.

READER'S TIP
Reading Minutes

- Use subheadings to guide your reading.
- Confirm the accuracy of any statements attributed to you.
- Double-check the description of decisions that affect your department

INCREASE READING SPEED

♦ Be Aggressive

Actively attack the material.

♦ Concentrate

Limit external and internal distractions.

♦ Stop Regressions

Be alert on the first reading.

♦ Use Pen as Pacer

Physically pull your eyes down the page.

9 CHAPTER NINE: ANALYTICAL REASONING

This chapter should be fun for the students while encouraging them to think. Discuss the characteristics of successful and unsuccessful students and emphasize the need to persistently and systematically work toward a problem's solution. Discuss how these characteristics apply to reading a textbook and to taking a test. Mention other test-taking clues that you have found helpful.

Students will enjoy working together in the introductory exercises. If they want more of these kinds of exercises, refer them to *Problem Solving and Comprehension* by Arthur Whimbey and Jack Lockhead (Philadelphia: Franklin Press, 1980).

READER'S TIP
Thinking about Maps, Charts, Graphs, and Diagrams

1. Read the title to determine the subject.
2. Read any information in italics or boldface.
3. Read the footnotes to determine the source of the information.
4. Read the labels to determine what each mark, arrow, figure, or design means.
5. Figure out the legend, the key on a map that shows what the markings represent.
6. Notice if numbers are written in some unit of measurement, such as percents, dollars, thousands, millions, or billions.
7. Notice the trends and the extremes. What is the average, and what are the highs and lows?
8. Refer back and forth to the text to follow a process or label parts.
9. Draw conclusions based on the information.
10. Do not read more into the illustration than is supported by fact. In other words, don't draw conclusions that cannot be proved.

READER'S TIP
Evaluating a Credit Card Offer

- How much is the annual fee for the card?
- What is the finance charge rate? Annual rates run 18%–22%, so finance charges can add up quickly.
- Does the rate start low and change after an initial introductory period? The balance may be subject to a higher interest rate after the initial period as the low rate expires.
- Why do you need it? If you already have one card, why do you need another one?

Selection 1: Hurricanes

Answer with T *(true) or* F *(false).*

Comprehension Quiz (for prereading or postreading)

F   1. The word *hurricane* is derived form the Hawaiian God of water.

F   2. Typhoons are more like tornadoes than hurricanes.

F   3. According to the passage most tropical disturbances reach hurricane status.

T   4. From the outside to the center of a hurricane, the barometric pressure drops.

T   5. The eye of the hurricane is the warmest part of the storm.

T   6. The eye of the hurricane is the calmest part of the storm.

F   7. Warm air decreases the strength of a hurricane.

F   8. Hurricanes usually build strength as they move across land.

T   9. Cold ocean waters decrease hurricane strength.

F   10. A storm surge refers to the wind from a hurricane.

Vocabulary Quiz (for prereading or postreading)

F   1. A tranquil evening is characterized by violence.

T   2. A ceiling fan cools by a rotary movement.

T   3. Sleet is a form of precipitation.

T   4. A basketball player can benefit from deceptive moves on the court.

F   5. Liberated criminals report to jail for imprisonment.

T   6. Look aloft to see clouds or stars.

F   7. A barrage of ammunition is a single deadly shot.

F   8. A scheduled airplane departure is an example of flying debris.

T   9. Torrential rains are rains that are heavier than usual.

T   10. The advent of a holiday season is the beginning rather than the end.

Selection 2: Obedience

Answer with T *(true) or* F *(false).*

Comprehension Quiz (for prereading or postreading)

T _____ 1. Subjects were told that they were part of an investigation to test the effects of punishment, in the form of electric shock, on memory.

T _____ 2. The learner, the person receiving the shock, was an actor.

F _____ 3. Milgram found that almost no one would deliver the full 450 volts.

F _____ 4. Personality tests revealed that subjects who delivered the voltage were vastly different from those who refused.

T _____ 5. Some of the subjects were shaking and weeping as they pressed the voltage lever.

Vocabulary Quiz (for prereading or postreading)

T _____ 1. When possible, administrators have underlings do the time-consuming jobs.

F _____ 2. A property adjacent to yours does not touch your property line.

T _____ 3. An ominous sound hints of misfortune.

T _____ 4. Legitimate orders are within the law.

F _____ 5. Anguish over a decision is pleasant and short-lived.

T _____ 6. Vividly describing an event usually gives a fairly clear picture to the listener.

T _____ 7. A communal bathroom lacks the privacy of one in a private home.

F _____ 8. In a trial, a lawyer usually likes to present an incomprehensible story to the judge.

T _____ 9. Mock apples are difficult to eat.

T _____ 10. A solitary flower blooms alone.

Selection 3: Business

Answer with T *(true) or* F *(false).*

Comprehension Quiz (for prereading or postreading)

F   ____   1. The author feels that motivation should come from the supervisor.

T   ____   2. Maltz was a plastic surgeon who observed positive changes in his patients after surgery.

T   ____   3. Self-fulfillment is the highest level on Maslow's hierarchy of needs.

T   ____   4. Gellerman believes that you should work for the organization and yourself at the same time.

T   ____   5. Motivation-seekers usually achieve more than maintenance-seekers.

Vocabulary Quiz (for prereading or postreading)

T   ____   1. Too much supervision can make an employee feel stifled.

T   ____   2. An inspired worker wants to achieve a goal.

F   ____   3. The proponent of a cause is firmly against it.

T   ____   4. If you operate on a premise, you have some basis for drawing conclusions.

T   ____   5. To reach the pinnacle of success is considered the highest level of achievement.

F   ____   6. The crux of an issue is an insignificant detail.

T   ____   7. A de-emphasis on college language study would probably mean fewer language requirements for graduation.

F   ____   8. A sociologist is primarily concerned with personal hygienics.

T   ____   9. Grievances are complaints that are made by workers.

T   ____   10. Verbalizing a problem can be a way of relieving the tension.

New Skill

The author would support the first four options. The remaining six offer very little. Some, in fact, could do more harm than good.

Norman works for a company that has many advantages. He might not improve his situation elsewhere. His first step, therefore, is to motivate himself. If his attitude improves, he will be more likely to be considered for a better role. Norman should then talk with his supervisor about assuming more responsibility. He might get some assistance, perhaps psychological support, from a discussion with the right person.

When an employee becomes dissatisfied or reaches a plateau it is always a good idea to search for another role with another company. There are two reasons for this: (1) the individual can thus find out whether or not he (or she) can really improve himself—instead of just thinking about it—and (2) searching for a better role often motivates the person in his present job because it helps him get out of a mental rut. It can also make him see more clearly the advantages (or disadvantages) of his present job.

 # CHAPTER TEN: INFERENCE

As you present Chapter Ten, discuss the situations in which students already use inferential comprehension skills in everyday life. Ask them to bring in jokes to share with the class. Talk about the implied meaning in each joke and what makes the joke funny.

Advertisements are fun to use when teaching implied meaning. Cigarette and liquor advertisements are particularly interesting to include in a class discussion because they are trying to sell products that are basically unhealthy.

Sensitize students to the political manipulation of phrases with a positive connotation. Ask students to write a speech stating a position on an issue and using the following phrases. Discuss the familiarity of the phrases and the impact. Why do politicians use such phrases? How effective are they?

Use Positive Connotation for Political Spin

Create a political speech stating your position on a national issue. Weave the following phrases into your speech:

New attitude

Bet on the future

Strengthen the American family

Empower Americans to make decisions for their own lives

Right choice for the country

New approach for America

Important moment for the country

How America is meant to be

Good sound judgment for the people

Come together and do what is right for the people

READER'S TIP
Reading and Studying a Speech or Essay

Ask yourself the following questions:

- What is the theme, thesis, or main idea?
- How do the details and examples develop the theme?
- How does the title aid in understanding the essay?
- What is the author's attitude toward the subject?
- What images contribute to the theme of the essay?
- What is the conclusion? How is it significant?

READER'S TIP
Reading Editorials

- What event prompted the editorial?
- What is the thesis or opinion being promoted by the author?
- Do the details prove the thesis?
- Is the author liberal or conservative?
- What is left out?
- Are the sources, facts, and other support credible?

Selection 1: Commencement Address: Living Up to Your Fullest Potential

Answer with T *(true) or* F *(false).*

Comprehension Quiz (for prereading or postreading)

F ____ 1. The speech is written by a student.

F ____ 2. In the anecdote, the elephant pulls the stake out of the ground.

F ____ 3. In the story, the student with the major mishaps did not get her internship.

F ____ 4. In the story, the student's GPA was affected by 10% by the mishap.

F ____ 5. In the report by the National Alliance of Business, high school graduates earn approximately 15% more than nongraduates.

T ____ 6. The author states that she has found inner strength for a "nest egg."

F ____ 7. Mother Theresa's quote states that the fruit is at the end of the limb.

T ____ 8. The speaker refers back to the words of her own commencement speaker for a definition.

F ____ 9. The Irish proverb refers to building a sense of self.

T ____ 10. The author addresses the topics of both potential and community.

Selection 2: The Alchemist's Secret

Answer with T *(true) or* F *(false).*

Comprehension Quiz (for prereading or postreading)

T _____ 1. The author implies that Pechkoff, the foreign diplomat, had his first wife killed.

T _____ 2. The wife in the story who eats the chocolates was seeing a younger man and wanted a settlement.

T _____ 3. An autopsy is done to discover the cause of death.

F _____ 4. The husband and Pechkoff were business partners.

T _____ 5. The wife reached Dr. Maximus before the husband.

Selection 3: The Doctor's Heroism

Answer with T *(true) or* F *(false).*

Comprehension Quiz (for prereading or postreading)

F   _____ 1. The patients were not required to pay for the doctor's services.

T   _____ 2. The patients stripped to the waist to see the doctor.

T   _____ 3. The doctor told the millionaire patient to eat watercress.

F   _____ 4. The millionaire's treatment lasted for one year.

F   _____ 5. The doctor required the millionaire patient to schedule a return visit.

F   _____ 6. The patient went to Rome for the prescribed treatment.

T   _____ 7. The doctor asked if the patient was rich before telling him about the watercress treatment.

F   _____ 8. The doctor expressed belief in the prescribed treatment in order to motivate the patient.

F   _____ 9. The doctor prescribed the treatment in order to get the patient's fortune.

F   _____ 10. The doctor was angry at the patient and thus killed him.

Vocabulary Quiz (for prereading or postreading)

F   _____ 1. An indispensible employee is not essential to the business.

F   _____ 2. A cavernous landspace is flat and dry.

T   _____ 3. An eminent scientist is well known and respected.

F   _____ 4. To brusquely reply is to respond politely.

F   _____ 5. A dubious plan should generate commitment and trust.

F   _____ 6. A sanctum of color is a rainbow of light.

F   _____ 7. A wan complexion signals health and strength.

T   _____ 8. A beatific occasion suggests angels rather than devils.

T   _____ 9. A nominal fee is usually a small amount.

T   _____ 10. Sublime motives are noble rather than selfish.

 # CHAPTER ELEVEN: CRITICAL READING

Teaching students to read critically is to teach them to see beyond the printed page. Discuss how a particular author's interpretation can affect different types of college textbooks. It would be interesting to have conflicting opinions of a historical figure from two historians as an example.

Newspaper editorials are also useful for teaching critical reading. Collect a few that are funny. Share some of these with your students and talk about how the writers say one thing but mean another. For an assignment, ask students to bring in an editorial and answer the following questions about it:

- **Purpose or intent:** Why did the author write the article?
- **Bias or point of view:** What side does the author take on the subject (for or against)?
- **Main idea (implied meaning):** What point is the author trying to make?
- **Background knowledge:** What do you need to know to understand the editorial?
- **Tone:** What is the feeling or mood of the passage? (examples: sarcastic, angry, sympathetic, humorous)

CRITICAL READERS

♦ Distinguish Fact from Opinion

Proven true or false

Feeling

♦ Recognize Slanted Language

Connotation

Slant

♦ Recognize the Author's Point of View

Writer's position on topic

Author's perspective or view

♦ Recognize Biases

Author's bias

Reader's bias

♦ Recognize the Author's Tone

Attitude toward subject

Relates to tone of voice

READER'S TIP
Recognizing the Author's Tone

The following list of words with explanations can describe an author's tone or attitude:

Absurd, farcical, ridiculous: laughable or a joke

Ambivalent, apathetic, detached: not caring

Angry, bitter, hateful: feeling bad and upset about the topic

Arrogant, condescending: acting conceited or above others

Awestruck, admiring, wondering: filled with wonder

Cheerful, joyous, happy: feeling good about the topic

Compassionate, sympathetic: feeling sorrow at the distress of others

Complex: intricate, complicated, and entangled with confusing parts

Congratulatory, celebratory: honoring an achievement or festive occasion

Cruel, malicious: mean spirited

Cynical: expecting the worst from people

Depressed, melancholy: sad, dejected, or having low spirits

Disapproving: judging unfavorably

Distressed: suffering strain, misery, or agony

Evasive, abstruse: avoiding or confusing the issue

Formal: using an official style

Frustrated: blocked from a goal

Gentle: kind or of a high social class

Ghoulish, grim: robbing graves or feeding on corpses; stern and forbidding

Hard: unfeeling, strict, and unrelenting

Humorous, jovial, comic, playful, amused: being funny

Incredulous: unbelieving

Indignant: outraged

Intense, impassioned: extremely involved, zealous, or agitated

Ironic: the opposite of what is expected; a twist at the end

Irreverent: lack of respect for authority

Mocking, scornful, caustic, condemning: ridiculing the topic

Objective, factual, straightforward, critical: using facts without emotions

Obsequious: fawning for attention

Optimistic: looking on the bright side

Outspoken: speaking one's mind on issues

(Continued on next page)

Pathetic: moving one to compassion or pity

Pessimistic: looking on the negative side

Prayerful: religiously thankful

Reticent: shy and not speaking out

Reverent: showing respect

Righteous: morally correct

Romantic, intimate, loving: expressing love or affection

Sarcastic: saying one thing and meaning another

Satiric: using irony, wit, and sarcasm to discredit or ridicule

Sensational: over-dramatized or over-hyped

Sentimental, nostalgic: remembering the good old days

Serious, sincere, earnest, solemn: being honest and concerned

Straightforward: forthright

Subjective, opinionated: expressing opinions and feelings

Tragic: regrettable or deplorable mistake

Uneasy: restless or uncertain

Vindictive: seeking revenge

READER'S TIP
Critically Evaluating Electronic Material

Ask the following questions to evaluate:

- What are the author's credentials in the field? Is the author affiliated with a university? Check this by noting professional titles in the preface or introduction, finding a biographical reference in the library, or searching the Internet for additional references to the same author.

- Who paid for the Web page? Check the homepage for an address, as well as the end of the electronic address for *edu, gov, org,* or *com*. Depending on the material, this could lend credibility or raise further questions.

- What is the purpose of the Web page? Is the purpose to educate or to sell a product, a service, or an idea? Check the links to investigate the any hidden agendas.

- How do the biases of the author and the sponsor affect the material? Is the reasoning sound? Check the tone, assumptions, and evidence. What opposing views have been left out?

Selection 1: As They Say, Drugs Kill

Answer with T *(true) or* F *(false).*

Comprehension Quiz (for prereading or postreading)

F   _____   1. The people at the party no longer do drugs.

F   _____   2. The author's boyfriend was the one who died.

T   _____   3. The author's friend feels that the victim had a heart attack.

F   _____   4. The paramedics were never told about the drugs.

F   _____   5. The author feels the victim's death has made a difference to others contemplating drugs.

Vocabulary Quiz (for prereading or postreading)

T   _____   1. Her refusal to vote showed her ambivalence toward the candidates.

T   _____   2. A stupefied person rarely thinks clearly.

T   _____   3. Beginning to convulse signals the need for medical attention.

F   _____   4. A miraculous recovery is easily predictable.

F   _____   5. Speaking audibly means that you are not heard.

T   _____   6. Gnashing brakes probably indicates the need for auto repair.

T   _____   7. An irreverent teenager might yell at his mother.

T   _____   8. A freak accident takes an unnatural turn.

T   _____   9. Speculation on prices seldom keeps them stable.

F   _____   10. A casualty of battle is the soldier who comes home.

Selection 2: Women Selecting Names

Answer with T *(true) or* F *(false).*

Comprehension Quiz (for prereading or postreading)

F   ____   1. The four letters were from two males and two females.

F   ____   2. The author from Puerto Rico uses her husband's last name as her last name.

F   ____   3. In the case of Amy Verstappen, both her husband and her daughter took her last name.

T   ____   4. Spencer Clayton, the author of the last letter, lived with his mother after his parents divorced.

T   ____   5. Spencer Clayton wants his child to have his last name.

Vocabulary Quiz (for prereading or postreading)

T   ____   1. You can listen to a litany during a church service.

T   ____   2. A vestige is something that is left over form the past.

T   ____   3. Historians harken back to recall past times.

T   ____   4. A veiled insult is implied rather than directly stated.

F   ____   5. The mother is the dominant figure in a patriarchal society.

T   ____   6. Rhyming verses differentiate hip hop from jazz.

T   ____   7. You might need to interrupt to interject your thoughts into a heated conversation.

F   ____   8. Abortion is seldom considered a controversial issue.

T   ____   9. Virtually clean means most of the work has been completed.

F   ____   10. A scarring event of childhood quickly fades from memory and significance.

Selection 3: The Job Makes the Person

Answer with T *(true) or* F *(false).*

Comprehension Quiz (for prereading or postreading)

T ____ 1. The author found that blocked opportunity was a greater factor than gender in measuring ambition in business.

T ____ 2. The author feels that being well-liked is more important to dead-end workers than to ambitious corporate climbers.

F ____ 3. According to the passage, people who work for a woman boss are less likely to want another woman boss.

T ____ 4. The author feels that the most important distinguishing factor between a good and a bad boss is access to power in an organization.

T ____ 5. The author agrees with the findings of the 1965 *Harvard Business Review* survey.

Vocabulary Quiz (for prereading or postreading)

F ____ 1. The military structure is based on a disdain for power.

T ____ 2. Conventional wisdom is the traditionally accepted thought.

T ____ 3. Employers seek to hire competent people.

F ____ 4. An apparent problem is unlikely to appear.

F ____ 5. To shun fame is to seek the spotlight.

T ____ 6. People who have clout have a reputation for getting things done.

T ____ 7. Military rank distinguishes different echelons of power.

T ____ 8. Expertise can come from talent as well as from practice.

F ____ 9. To flounder in pursuit is to speed up the pace.

F ____ 10. A relentless enemy is easily lost.

CHAPTER TWELVE: INDEPENDENT TEXTBOOK ASSIGNMENTS

In order to model the thinking and processing of information needed for textbook learning, study aids have been included at the beginning of each of these three independent assignments. You may want to assist students or let them work independently. You may choose to do portions of each or an entire selection together to demonstrate the application of the skills learned throughout the text.

These three selections do not have to be used at the end of the course. You may want to space them out during the course to assist and monitor student progress. The selections are longer than previous ones to give students an opportunity for extended reading and study.

Help students organize their study according to the three stages of reading. Tell them what you expect in both process and outcome. For most students, annotation alone is not sufficient for successful mastery of the material. Encourage students to annotate first and then use some other form of organizing the information.

The tests for each selection vary in length but include multiple-choice or true-false items as well as an essay question. You may want to use some of the items in a classroom discussion and test with the remainder. Other options would be to use the essay questions as part of the study process, as a group project, or as a homework rather than a classwork assignment. Think creatively, and help students enjoy the application of their skills.

Independent Assignment 1: Conflict Management

Objective Exam

Answer the following with a, b, c, *or* d, *or* T *(true) or* F *(false).*

d _____ 1. The author believes that conflict
   a. rarely occurs between caring people.
   b. inevitably fosters suspicion.
   c. happens repeatedly in insignificant relationships.
   d. usually occurs in meaningful relationships.

c _____ 2. Examples of content conflict would include to all of the following except
   a. which television show to watch.
   b. how to spend money.
   c. who has the right to establish rules of behavior.
   d. whether an exam is fair.

b _____ 3. Louis and Tiffany had an argument over money and family budgeting. Louis left the house saying he wanted to drive around, calm down, and would probably not be back that night. Louis was engaging in
   a. force.
   b. avoidance.
   c. beltlining.
   d. win-lose.

c _____ 4. Whenever Maria failed to do a chore or came home late, her mother became angry and reminded Maria of her poor report card, her sloppy room, and her traffic ticket. Her mother was responding to conflict by
   a. force.
   b. avoidance.
   c. gunnysacking.
   d. argumentativeness.

c _____ 5. The author implies that ironically many victims of violence
   a. face the problems openly.
   b. tend to fight back aggressively.
   c. blame themselves for the problems.
   d. affix blame accurately.

c   _____ 6. The response tactic of personal rejection includes all of the following *except*

     a. demoralization.

     b. withdrawal of affection.

     c. face-enhancing tactics.

     d. inflicting feeling of self-worth.

a   _____ 7. The author view all of the following tactics as negative *except*

     a. argumentativeness.

     b. beltlining.

     c. avoidance.

     d. gunnysacking.

c   _____ 8. The includes all of the following *except*

     a. demoralization.

     b. withdrawal of affection.

     c. face-enhancing tactics.

     d. inflicting feeling of self-worth.

d   _____ 9. As they drive to the celebration, Yvonne discusses the reasons she is angry with Anthony about the upcoming birthday party. Anthony repeats his position on the issue, and Yvonne reminds Anthony that he just got fired from his job. Yvonne is engaging in

     a. avoidance.

     b. win-lose.

     c. personal rejection.

     d. beltlining.

Answer the following with T *(true) or* F *(false).*

T   _____ 10. According to the passage, an argument over which stereo to buy would most likely be considered a content conflict.

T   _____ 11. The author believes that confronting a concern usually means that the relationship is worth the effort.

F   _____ 12. The interdependence in interpersonal conflict refers to the independence that each person has as a separate individual.

T   _____ 13. Refusing to accept a parent's curfew time is a relational conflict.

T   _____ 14. Culture influences both the issues that people argue about and the strategies that people use when arguing.

F ____ 15. The author advises that a witness is needed when arguing with a partner.

F ____ 16. A compromise between two people is an example of a win-lose solution.

T ____ 17. The author suggests that including statements in an argument that begin with "Everybody thinks you're wrong about..." is a method of shifting of responsibility.

T ____ 18. According to the passage, a study found that almost 50% of a sample college students reported some experience of violence in a dating relationship.

T ____ 19. Face-detracting strategies embarrass and damage the ego of the other person.

T ____ 20. The author suggests that a beltlining tactic can cause serious injury that could terminate the relationship.

Essay Question

If you were teaching conflict resolution strategies to students, what strategies would you tell them to avoid and to embrace? Describe each strategy that you would tell them to avoid and give and example. Do the same for the strategies that you would tell them to use.

Study Outline: Conflict Management

I. Factors in interpersonal conflict

  A. People are interdependent

  B. Perceive goals to be incompatible

  C. Each interfering with goal achievement of other

II. Content and relationship conflicts

  A. Content conflicts

    1. Centers on objects, relationships, and people

    2. Ex.: what to watch on TV

  B. Relational conflicts

    1. Issues between people

    2. Ex.: who is in charge

III. Characteristics of conflict

  A. Part of every relationship

  B. Means you feel the relationship is worth the effort

  C. Cultural changes in issues and tactics

IV. Before and after conflict

  A. Before

    1. Try to fight in private.

    2. Choose time free of other problems.

    3. Know what you are fighting about.

    4. Fight about problems that can be solved.

  B. After

    1. Learn from conflict and process.

    2. Keep conflict in perspective.

    3. Attack your negative feelings.

    4. Increase the exchange of rewards and cherishing behaviors.

V. Seven strategies for conflict management

  A. Win-lose and win-win strategies

    1. One person wins and the other loses in win-lose solution.

    2. Both compromise and win in win-win solutions.

B. Avoidance
   1. Physical flight such as walking out
   2. Physical barrier such as blasting radio
   3. Emotional or intellectual avoidance such as not talking
   4. Take responsibility with your own I-messages
C. Force and talk
   1. Winner exerts most force
   2. Physical violence rate over 50% in studies
   3. Victims see violence as love and blame themselves
D. Gunnysacking
   1. Storing up grievances and unloading at one time
   2. Focus conflict on here-and-now.
E. Face-enhancing and face-detracting strategies
   1. Face-detracting: attack to embarrass and damage ego
   2. Face-enhancing: help other person retain a positive face
F. Attack and acceptance
   1. Personal rejection: withhold love and affection and demoralize to get way
   2. Beltlining: hitting below the belt to inflict harm
G. Verbal aggressiveness and argumentativeness
   1. Verbal aggressiveness: win by inflicting psychological pain
   2. Argumentativeness: willingness to argue for point of view and be productive
      a. Avoid assuming you are being attacked as a person.
      b. Avoid attacking the other person rather than the argument.
      c. Center arguments on issues rather than people.
      d. Reaffirm other person's sense of competence.
      e. Allow other person to save face.
      f. Avoid interrupting.
      g. Stress areas of agreement.
      h. Express interest in the other person's position.

Independent Assignment 2: The Surge Westward

Objective Exam

Answer with T *(true) or* F *(false).*

T   _____   1.   Members of the Donner party left for California with their wagons loaded with necessities and luxuries.

T   _____   2.   The Donner party decided to take a short cut to California rather than follow the original plan.

F   _____   3.   Being blocked by huge mountain boulders was the primary reason the Donner party pioneers were unable to cross the Truckee Pass.

F   _____   4.   The surviving Donner party members were trapped in Truckee for less than a month.

T   _____   5.   Of the 17 men and women of the Donner party who left Truckee to find help in a settlement, only seven survived.

T   _____   6.   The Donner party survivors who left Truckee for help shot and ate two Native-American guides.

F   _____   7.   Of the original 87 members of the Donner party, only 27 survived.

T   _____   8.   The initials "GTT" painted on the gate of a home meant the residents had "Gone to Texas."

F   _____   9.   Thomas Jefferson appointed Lewis and Clark because of their previous jobs as explorers.

T   _____ 10.   Lewis and Clark traveled along the Columbia river to the Pacific Ocean.

F   _____ 11.   Lewis and Clark described the Great Plains as a "Great American Desert."

T   _____ 12.   Zebulon Pike explored the southern portion of the Louisiana territory.

F   _____ 13.   The Rocky Mountain Fur Company preferred to buy skins from Native Americans.

F   _____ 14.   The "rendezvous system" was established to insure the safety of the trappers.

F   _____ 15.   The Santa Fe and Oregon trails were first developed by the government to be used by settlers moving west in wagon trains.

F   _____ 16.   John Bidwell opened the Santa Fe Trail.

F ____ 17. The first party of 69 pioneers that left Missouri for California did not encounter the massive hardships of pioneers who followed the next year.

F ____ 18. The term "manifest destiny" was coined by Thomas Jefferson.

F ____ 19. Gender roles remained distinct on the wagon trains westward.

T ____ 20. Manifest destiny is the romantic notion that God meant for Americans to over-spread the continent.

Essay Question

Explain the cause and effect nature of the sequence of westward expansion. Give details about the motivations and accomplishments of the explorers, the traders, and the settlers.